CHOCOLATE RECIPES

Cakes, Puddings and Sweets

with illustrations by
James Mathews, William Affleck
and other artists

SALMON

Index

Cover pictures: *front:* A Cottage Door. *Back:* A Cottage Garden
Title page: Hollyhocks *by James Matthews*

Rich Chocolate Cake

A traditional, light chocolate sponge recipe.

6 oz flour
6 oz caster sugar
5 oz butter or margarine
1½ oz cocoa powder
Pinch of salt
3 eggs, separated
Vanilla essence
Chocolate Icing (*page 45*)

Set oven to 375°F or Mark 5. Butter and flour a 6 inch round cake tin. Sieve the flour into a bowl together with the cocoa powder and salt. Separate the eggs. Put the butter or margarine into a warm bowl and work it with a wooden spoon until it is creamy. Beat in the sugar, add the egg yolks then stir in the dry ingredients. Whip the egg whites stiffly and fold into the mixture, as lightly as possible with a few drops of vanilla essence. Put into the tin and bake for about 1 hour 20 minutes or until a skewer inserted comes out clean. When cooked, turn out on a wire rack to cool. When cold, ice with Chocolate Icing and decorate with silver balls or crystallised violets.

Chocolate Meringues

The chocolate flavoured alternative to a basic home-made meringue.

2oz caster sugar	**Whites of 2 eggs**
½ oz cocoa powder	**2oz granulated sugar**

Set oven as low as possible; just warm. Line baking sheets with baking parchment. Sieve together the caster sugar and cocoa powder. Separate the yolks from the whites of egg and beat the whites stiffly in a bowl. Whisk in the granulated sugar and then fold in the sugar/cocoa mixture as lightly as possible with a metal spoon so as to retain the air bubbles in the egg whites. Spoon very gently on to the baking sheets (using two dessertspoons), allowing room for the meringues to spread. Put into the warm oven and cook for several hours until the meringues are quite dry and firm. Leave to cool on the baking sheets before removing, very gently, and then sandwich together with whipped cream.

Chocolate Coconut Kisses

A melt-in-the-mouth chocolate coconut sweetmeat.

2½ oz cocoa powder
1 lb icing sugar
2 oz desiccated coconut
3 tablespoons unsweetened evaporated milk
White of 1 egg

Mix together in a bowl the cocoa powder, icing sugar and desiccated coconut. Stir in the 3 tablespoons of evaporated milk. Beat the egg white stiffly and then fold into the mixture with a metal spoon. Well dust the hands with icing sugar, take teaspoons of the mixture and roll into small, equal size balls. Place the balls on a tray lined with greaseproof paper and set aside in a warm place for several hours to dry out thoroughly.

Chocolate Viennoise Pudding

A rich, fruity steamed chocolate pudding.

5 oz bread (crusts removed)
3 oz caster sugar
2½ fl.oz water
½ pint hot milk
2 dessertspoons plain drinking chocolate
2 eggs, beaten
2 oz candied peel
3 oz sultanas
2 oz glacé cherries, halved
Juice and grated rind of ½ lemon
Wineglass medium sherry (optional)
2 tablespoons single cream (optional)
Chocolate Sauce (*page 43*)

Well butter a 6 inch pudding basin. Cut the bread into very small pieces. Put the sugar and water into a heavy saucepan and cook until it becomes light, golden brown. Stir in the hot milk. When the caramel has dissolved, stir in the chocolate. Beat the eggs in a basin, pour on to them the milk mixture and whisk for a few minutes. Put the diced bread, candied peel, sultanas, glacé cherries and grated lemon rind into a mixing bowl and pour on the milk mixture. Mix well, adding the lemon juice and the sherry and cream (if preferred). Cover and seal with kitchen foil and steam for about 2 hours, topping up the water as necessary. Serve with Chocolate Sauce. Serves 4-6.

Chocolate Creole Biscuits

Chocolate-shortbread sandwich biscuits.

2 oz plain drinking chocolate
1 tablespoon milk
4 oz flour
Pinch of salt
3 oz butter
1 oz sugar
1 egg, beaten
½ teaspoon vanilla essence
Chocolate Butter Icing (*page 45*)
Chocolate Icing (*page 45*)

Set oven to 350ºF or Mark 4. Grease and flour a baking sheet. In a cup, dissolve the chocolate powder in the milk. Sieve the flour and salt into a bowl and rub in the butter until the mixture resembles fine breadcrumbs. Add the sugar then mix in the chocolate milk with a little beaten egg, finally adding the vanilla essence. Set the mixture aside for a short while until it becomes firm, then roll out fairly thinly on a floured surface. Cut into small rounds, about 1½ inch, with a cutter and set out on the baking sheet. Bake for about 15 minutes until golden, then transfer to a wire rack to cool. When the biscuits are cold, spread a little Chocolate Butter Icing on half the number and then place another biscuit on top. Finally ice each biscuit with Chocolate Icing.

Chocolate Toffee

A chocolate butter toffee recipe.

1 lb Demerara sugar
1 oz butter
1½ oz plain drinking chocolate
¼ pint water

Well butter a shallow tin about 12 inches by 8 inches. Put all the ingredients together into a saucepan over a low heat to melt, stirring all the time. When melted, bring to the boil and boil rapidly until 280°F/140°C on a sugar thermometer is reached or until a little of the mixture tested in cold water forms hard but not brittle threads. When ready, pour the mixture into the tin and leave to cool. When nearly cold, mark into squares with an oiled knife and, when quite cold, break into pieces. Wrap in kitchen foil, unless the toffee is to be eaten almost immediately.

Chocolate Date Cake

An unusual combination of chocolate and dates in this moist cake.

8 oz flour
1½ teaspoons baking powder
Pinch of salt
1½ oz plain drinking chocolate
2 tablespoons milk
3 oz dates
4 oz butter
5 oz sugar
2 small eggs, beaten

Set oven to 375°F or Mark 5. Grease and flour a 6 inch round cake tin. Sieve together into a bowl the flour, baking powder and salt. In a cup, dissolve the chocolate powder in the milk. Stone the dates and cut each one into two or three pieces. Rub the butter into the flour until it resembles breadcrumbs then add and mix in the dates and sugar. Make a well in the centre, add the beaten eggs and milk/chocolate mixture and mix well together to blend all the ingredients. Put into the tin and bake for about 1 hour or until a skewer inserted comes out clean. Transfer to a wire rack to cool.

Chocolate Almond Tart

An open tart topped with baked meringue.

4oz shortcrust pastry

FILLING

1oz butter	**1 tablespoon milk**
2½ oz caster sugar	**2 teaspoons cocoa powder**
Yolk of 1 egg	**3oz ground almonds**

½ teaspoon vanilla essence

MERINGUE

White of 1 egg 2oz sugar

Set oven to 375°F or Mark 5. Well grease a 6¾ inch sandwich tin. Roll out the pastry on a floured surface to about ¼ inch thick and line the tin. In a bowl, beat the butter to a cream with a wooden spoon, stir in the sugar then beat in the egg yolk and the milk. Mix together the cocoa powder and ground almonds, stir them into the mixture and lastly stir in the vanilla essence and blend well. Put the mixture into the lined tin and cook for 30 minutes. Make the meringue mixture by beating the egg white stiffly in a bowl and then fold in the sugar with a metal spoon. Ten minutes before the end of cooking time, remove the tart from the oven, cover the top with the meringue mixture and replace for the final 10 minutes. Allow to cool slightly in the tin before turning out. Serve with double cream.

Chocolate Parkin

A chocolate variation of a traditional Yorkshire ginger cake.

7 oz flour
2 tablespoons mixed spice
A little grated nutmeg
½ teaspoon bicarbonate of soda
2 oz cocoa powder
3 oz butter
5 oz fine or medium oatmeal
3 oz sugar
6 oz golden syrup, warmed
1 egg, beaten
½ pint milk

Set oven to 375°F or Mark 5. Grease and flour an 8 inch round or square cake tin. Sieve the flour into a bowl together with the mixed spice, nutmeg, bicarbonate of soda and cocoa powder. Rub in the butter until the mixture resembles fine breadcrumbs then stir in the oatmeal and sugar. Make a well in the centre and add the warmed syrup gradually, stirring, together with the beaten egg and milk a little at a time to produce a smooth mixture. Put into the tin and bake for 50 minutes or until a skewer inserted comes out clean. When cooked, leave in the tin for a few minutes then turn out on to a wire rack to cool.

Chocolate Coconut Buns

A simple recipe; a children's favourite.

8oz flour	**6oz caster sugar**
2oz cocoa powder	**1 egg**
1 teaspoon baking powder	**1oz desiccated coconut**
4oz butter	**½ teaspoon vanilla essence**

Milk to mix

Set oven to 375°F or Mark 5. Well butter small bun tins. Sieve together into a bowl the flour, cocoa powder and baking powder. In another bowl, beat the butter with a wooden spoon to cream it, add the sugar and beat in the egg. Next stir in the dry ingredients, including the desiccated coconut. Add the vanilla essence and sufficient milk, a little at a time, to mix to a stiff, dropping consistency. Put the mixture into the buttered tins and bake for 15 minutes. Turn out on to a wire rack to cool.

Chocolate Genoese Sponge

This recipe gives a really good, rich sponge which has the advantage of keeping fresh for several weeks. It is ideal for iced fancy cakes.

3 oz flour
2 teaspoons cocoa powder
3 eggs
4 oz sugar
3 oz butter

Set oven to 375°F or Mark 5. Line a flat tin approx 8 inches x 9 inches with baking parchment. Sieve together into a bowl the flour and cocoa powder. Put the eggs and sugar into a basin set in a saucepan of boiling water and whisk vigorously for about 10 to 15 minutes. In another pan, just melt the butter but do not allow to get hot. Remove any white curd from the top. Stir the melted butter gradually into the beaten eggs and sugar and then, very lightly, fold in the flour mixture. Blend thoroughly then pour into the tin and spread out evenly. Cook for 30 minutes or until a skewer inserted comes out clean. Turn out on a wire rack to cool. Finally cut into individual cakes and ice and decorate as preferred.

Chocolate Ginger Biscuits

A chocolate variation of a type of ginger fairing.

4oz flour
1 tablespoon cocoa powder
¼ teaspoon bicarbonate of soda
2 teaspoons ground ginger
2oz butter
1½ tablespoons golden syrup
2oz sugar

Set oven to 325°F or Mark 3. Grease a baking tray. Sieve together into a bowl the flour, cocoa powder, bicarbonate of soda and ground ginger. Put the butter and syrup into a saucepan and melt over a low heat, stirring, but do not allow to get hot. Add the sugar and, when dissolved, stir in the dry ingredients and beat hard. Allow to get cold then turn out the mixture on to a lightly floured surface and roll out to about ¼ inch thick. Cut out the biscuits with a 2 inch plain cutter and place on the baking tray. Bake for about 20 minutes and, when cooked and golden brown, place on a wire rack to cool.

Chocolate Tartlets

Individual tarts with a jam and chocolate filling.

4oz shortcrust pastry
Apricot jam

FILLING

2oz butter
2oz sugar
1 egg, separated
2 teaspoons cocoa powder
2oz ground rice
Vanilla essence
1 tablespoon milk

Set oven to 400°F or Mark 6. Grease deep patty tins. Roll out the pastry on a floured surface, cut out and line the tins, then put a teaspoon of jam in the bottom of each one. *Filling:* beat the butter and sugar together in a bowl until creamy, beat in the egg yolk, then fold in the sieved cocoa powder and ground rice. Add a few drops of vanilla essence. Beat the egg white stiffly and fold in as carefully as possible with a metal spoon. Then add a little milk to soften the mixture to a dropping consistency. Put 2 teaspoons of the mixture into each tart and bake for about 15 minutes until cooked and lightly browned. Turn out on a wire rack to cool.

Chocolate Gateau Delight

This recipe makes one of the most delicious sponge sandwiches.

6½ oz caster sugar	**5oz flour**
6 tablespoons water	**Chocolate Fudge Filling (*page 46*)**
3 eggs	**Chocolate Icing (*page 45*)**

Set oven to 375°F or Mark 5. Line an 8 inch sandwich tin with baking parchment. Put the sugar and water into a saucepan, bring slowly to the boil, stirring, then boil for about 3 minutes until syrupy. Allow to cool for about 3 minutes and, meantime, break the eggs into a basin and whip them. When the syrup mixture is cool, pour on to the beaten eggs and whisk until the mixture thickens. Sieve in the flour and fold lightly into the mixture. When well blended put into the tin, spread out and bake for about 45 minutes until lightly golden. Turn out on to a wire rack to cool. Then split in half, spread the bottom half with Chocolate Fudge Filling, replace the top half and then spread the top with Chocolate Icing.

Chocolate Madeleines

Small fancy cakes, baked in a mould, coated with jam and coconut and flavoured with chocolate.

4oz flour
1 level teaspoon baking powder
1oz cocoa powder
4oz sugar
4oz butter
2 eggs
Apricot jam
Desiccated coconut
Glacé cherries and angelica, to decorate

Set oven to 400°F or Mark 6. Well butter 10 to 12 individual, deep dariole moulds. Sieve together into a bowl the flour, baking powder and cocoa powder. In another bowl beat together the butter and sugar until creamy, then beat in each egg separately and then stir in the dry ingredients. Three parts fill each tin with the mixture and bake for about 15 minutes or until the cakes feel firm. Turn out on a wire rack to cool. Warm a little apricot jam. When the cakes are cold, brush each top and side with jam, holding on a skewer to do so. Then roll in the coconut and decorate the tops with half a glacé cherry and pieces of angelica.

Chocolate Shortbread

A traditional shortbread, flavoured with chocolate.

8oz flour
1½ oz cocoa powder
Pinch of salt
5oz butter
4oz caster sugar
Yolk of 1 egg

Set oven to 350ºF or Mark 4. Butter a 9 inch x 6 inch shallow tin. Sieve the flour, cocoa powder and salt into a bowl and mix well. Rub the butter into the flour mixture with the fingers, working in well. Stir in the sugar and mix with only just sufficient yolk of egg to make the mixture bind. Put the mixture into the tin, spread out and flatten with the fingers. Bake for one hour and, on removal from the oven, score with a knife into slices. Leave in the tin to get cold.

Chocolate Fudge Cake

A chocolate Madeira cake with chocolate fudge filling.

8 oz flour
2 oz cocoa powder
1½ teaspoons baking powder
3½ oz butter
7 oz caster sugar
3 eggs, separated
¼ pint milk
Almond essence
Chocolate Fudge Filling (*page 46*)
Icing sugar, for sprinkling

Set oven to 350ºF or Mark 4. Grease a shallow 8 inch x 12 inch baking tin. Sieve together into a bowl the flour, cocoa powder and baking powder. In another bowl beat the butter with a wooden spoon until it is creamy then beat in the sugar and the egg yolks. Stir in the mixed dry ingredients alternately with the milk, a little at a time. Finally, add a few drops of almond essence. Beat the egg whites stiffly and mix in as lightly as possible with a metal spoon. Put the mixture into the tin, spread out and bake for 50 minutes to 1 hour. Transfer to a wire rack to cool then spread with Chocolate Fudge Filling and sprinkle with icing sugar.

Chocolate Macaroons

A chocolate-flavoured tea time favourite.

1½oz cocoa powder
3½ tablespoons milk
White of 1 egg
8oz caster sugar
4oz ground almonds
Vanilla essence
Rice paper
Blanched almonds, split, to decorate

Set oven to 350ºF or Mark 4. First warm the milk and dissolve the cocoa powder in it thoroughly. Whip the egg white stiffly in a bowl, fold in the sugar and ground almonds and then the cocoa/milk mixture. Lastly add a few drops of vanilla essence. Place rice paper on a baking sheet and spoon on equal size heaps of the mixture, according to preference, leaving room for them to spread. Top each cake with a split almond. Bake for about 15 to 20 minutes until cooked and lightly browned and then transfer to a wire rack to cool.

Chocolate Banana Trifles

Individual desserts combining banana pieces and chocolate mousse.

2 or 3 bananas
Juice of ½ lemon
2 teaspoons powdered gelatine
½ pint water
2oz plain drinking chocolate
1oz sugar
Whites of 2 eggs
Vanilla essence
Chopped almonds and cream, to decorate

Slice the bananas and put pieces in the bottom of individual dessert glasses. Sprinkle with a little sugar and lemon juice. Put the water in a saucepan over a low heat and dissolve in it the gelatine powder, then add the chocolate powder and 1 oz sugar and dissolve slowly. When ready, turn into a basin and allow to cool. Whisk the egg whites stiffly in a bowl. When the chocolate mixture is nearly cold, add a few drops of vanilla essence and fold in the beaten egg whites with a metal spoon. Put sufficient of this mixture into each glass on the banana so as to reach the top and put in the refrigerator to set. When set, decorate the tops with chopped almonds and piped or drizzled cream.

Chocolate Meringue Pudding

A chocolate 'Queen of Puddings' recipe.

½ pint milk
3 oz sugar
1½ teaspoons cocoa powder
1 oz butter
2 oz breadcrumbs
2 eggs, separated

Set oven to 350°F or Mark 4. Grease a pie dish. Put the milk into a saucepan and add 1 oz of the sugar together with the cocoa powder and the butter. Bring to the boil and then pour on to the breadcrumbs in a mixing bowl. Allow to cool somewhat, then stir in the egg yolks. Put this mixture into the pie dish, spread out and bake until set. Meanwhile, whisk the egg whites very stiffly, adding the other 2 ozs of the sugar. When the pie is cooked, pile the meringue mixture on top. Lower the oven temperature and return the pudding to a cool oven until the meringue is set and pale golden brown in colour. Serves 4.

Chocolate Walnut Fudge

Deliciously nutty and chewy, with a rich chocolate flavour.

1lb granulated sugar
½ pint evaporated milk, unsweetened
1oz plain drinking chocolate
1oz butter
2 tablespoons cocoa powder
3oz chopped walnuts

Well butter a rectangular tin about 10 inches by 7 inches. Put all the ingredients, except the walnuts, into a heavy saucepan. Heat slowly over a low heat until a temperature of 238°F/114°C on a sugar thermometer is reached or until a little of the mixture dropped into cold water forms a soft ball when rolled between the finger and thumb. Stir in the walnuts, beat until the mixture becomes thick and creamy and then pour at once into the tin and spread out. When cold and set, cut into convenient size squares and store in an airtight tin.

Chocolate Sponge Roll

A light, fat-free chocolate sponge roll.

4 oz flour
1 oz cocoa powder
Pinch of baking powder
3 eggs
5 oz caster sugar
Vanilla essence
Apricot jam
Icing sugar, for sprinkling

Set oven to 425ºF or Mark 7. Line a 13 inch x 9 inch Swiss Roll tin with baking parchment. Sieve the flour into a bowl together with the cocoa powder and baking powder. In another bowl, whisk together the eggs and sugar until pale in colour, light and frothy. Fold into the flour mixture as lightly as possible, with a few drops of vanilla essence and blend well. Put into the tin and bake for 8 minutes. Turn out on to a sheet of baking paper which has been well dusted with sugar and trim the edges. Spread the cake with warmed apricot jam and roll up very carefully, off the paper, into a neat roll. Transfer to a wire rack to cool. When cold, sprinkle with icing sugar. Alternatively, if preferred, ice with Chocolate Butter Icing.

Chocolate Almond Cake

A Madeira-type chocolate cake flavoured with almonds.

6 oz flour
2 teaspoons cocoa powder
1 oz ground almonds
½ teaspoon baking powder
Pinch of salt
3 oz butter
5 oz caster sugar
2 eggs, separated
¼ pint milk
Almond essence
1 oz blanched almonds, split

Set oven to 375°F or Mark 5. Grease and flour a 6 inch round cake tin. Sieve together into a bowl the flour, cocoa powder, ground almonds, baking powder and a pinch of salt. In another bowl, beat the butter with a wooden spoon until it is creamy then add the sugar and blend well together. Beat the egg yolks into the mixture then stir in the mixed dry ingredients alternately with the milk, a little at a time. Finally, add a few drops of almond essence. Beat the egg whites stiffly and fold in as lightly as possible with a metal spoon. Put the mixture into the tin, cover the top with the split almonds and bake for about 1 hour 10 minutes or until a skewer inserted comes out clean. Transfer to a wire rack to cool.

Chocolate and Orange Loaf

A plain, orange-flavoured chocolate cake.

¾ lb wholemeal flour
¼ teaspoon salt
2 oz cocoa powder
3 teaspoons baking powder
3 oz butter or margarine
4 oz sugar
Grated rind of 2 oranges and the juice of 1 orange
Milk to mix (approx ½ pint)

Set oven to 375°F or Mark 5. Butter and flour an 8 inch round cake tin. Sieve the flour into a bowl together with the salt, cocoa powder and baking powder. Rub in the fat until the mixture resembles fine breadcrumbs then stir in the sugar and grated orange rind. Mix with the orange juice and sufficient milk to make a dropping mixture; the amount of milk will depend on the absorption of the flour. Put into the tin and bake for about ¾ hour until firm to the touch or until a skewer inserted comes out clean. When cooked, turn out on to a wire rack to cool.

Chocolate Eclairs

Small, finger-shaped cakes of choux pastry, filled with whipped cream and topped with chocolate icing.

2oz butter	**3 small or medium eggs**
¼ pint boiling water	**Whipped cream**
4oz flour	**Chocolate Icing (*page 45*)**

Set oven to 400ºF or Mark 6. Grease a baking tray. Put the butter into a saucepan over a low heat, add the boiling water then stir in the flour and beat hard until the mixture is thick and smooth and leaves the side of the pan. Remove the pan from the heat and allow to cool slightly. Add the unbeaten eggs one at a time, beating the mixture thoroughly until smooth before adding the next one. The eggs should be absolutely fresh. If very large, 2½ eggs may be sufficient. Put the paste into an icing bag with a ½ inch plain round nozzle and pipe strips 3 - 4 inches long on the baking tray. Bake for 25-30 minutes according to size. When cold make a slit in the side of each eclair and fill with whipped cream. Coat the tops with Chocolate Icing.

Chocolate Coconut Cake

A plain chocolate cake, covered with chocolate icing and coated with desiccated coconut.

6 oz flour
1½ oz cocoa powder
1 teaspoon baking powder
3 oz desiccated coconut
3 oz butter
3 oz caster sugar
1 egg
¼ pint milk
Chocolate Icing (*page 45*)
Desiccated coconut, to decorate

Set oven to 325° or Mark 3. Grease and line a 6 inch round cake tin. Sieve together into a bowl the flour, cocoa powder and baking powder and add the desiccated coconut. In another bowl beat the butter with a wooden spoon until it is creamy, then beat in the caster sugar and the egg. Stir in the mixed dry ingredients alternately with the milk, a little at a time. Put the mixture into the tin, make a hollow in the centre and bake for 1¼ hours or until a skewer inserted comes out clean. Transfer to a wire rack to cool, then coat the top and side with Chocolate Icing and then cover the side of the cake with desiccated coconut.

Chocolate Truffles

A rich, chocolate and coconut sweetmeat which can be served as a 'petit four'.

¼ lb best quality plain block chocolate
2oz icing sugar
1½ tablespoons evaporated milk, unsweetened
½ teaspoon vanilla essence
Desiccated coconut

Melt the chocolate in a basin over a pan of hot water, but do not allow to get hot. When melted, stir in the icing sugar, evaporated milk and vanilla essence and blend thoroughly together. No cooking is required so, next, shape into small balls by rolling in the hands and then roll each ball in the desiccated coconut to coat all over. These truffles can be kept in an airtight tin in the refrigerator for up to 3 days.

Chocolate Cabinet Pudding

This is an excellent way of using up stale cake or cake trimmings and also left-over cake slices.

Cake crumbs
1oz glacé cherries, halved
2oz sultanas
1oz sugar
Grated rind of ½ lemon
½ pint milk
2 dessertspoons plain drinking chocolate
2 eggs, beaten

Well butter a 5 inch pudding basin and decorate the bottom with a few glacé cherries. Into a mixing bowl crush sufficient cake crumbs as will three-quarters fill the basin. Mix with the crumbs the remaining glacé cherries, the sultanas, sugar and grated lemon rind. Put the milk into a saucepan over a low heat and stir in the chocolate powder. When hot, but not boiling, pour the milk on to the beaten eggs in a basin. Whisk for a few seconds then pour the milk on to the cake crumbs and stir until the milk and dry ingredients are well mixed. Put the mixture into the pudding basin, cover and seal with kitchen foil and steam for 1 hour and 10 minutes, topping up the water as necessary. Turn out and serve, either by itself or with custard or cream.

Chocolate Log Cake

A plain sponge roll with apricot jam filling and covered with chocolate butter cream icing.

4 oz flour
1 level teaspoon baking powder
Pinch of salt
2 oz butter
4 oz sugar
2 eggs
A little milk
Apricot jam
Chocolate Butter Icing (*page 45*)

Set oven to 400ºF or Mark 6. Grease a Swiss Roll tin. Sieve together into a bowl the flour, baking powder and salt. In another bowl, beat the butter with a wooden spoon until it is creamy then add the sugar and each egg separately, beating in hard. Stir in the mixed dry ingredients alternately with just a little milk, some at a time. Put the mixture into the tin and bake for 9 to 10 minutes until lightly cooked. Turn out on to a sheet of baking paper which has been well dusted with sugar. Spread the cake with warmed apricot jam and roll up very carefully, off the paper, into a neat roll. Transfer to a wire rack to cool. Trim the ends and spread all over with Chocolate Butter Icing and mark with a fork to represent tree bark.

Chocolate Mint Shake

3 oz plain drinking chocolate
8 fl. oz water
2 pints milk
4 oz sugar
½ teaspoon peppermint essence
½ pint vanilla ice cream

In a pan, dissolve the chocolate in the water over a low heat, then add the milk and sugar and stir. Simmer for 5 minutes then remove from the heat and allow to cool somewhat. Stir in the peppermint essence and set aside to get cold. When quite cold, whisk in the ice cream and transfer to a large serving jug. Put into the refrigerator if the drink is not to be served immediately. Serve in tall glasses.

Chocolate Egg Nogg

1 cup milk
1 heaped teaspoon cocoa powder
1 egg, separated
1 teaspoon cream (if available)

Blend the cocoa powder with a little cold milk. Put with the remaining milk into a pan, bring to the boil and boil for about 2 to 3 minutes. Put the egg yolk into a basin and pour in the milk, whisking while pouring. Beat the white of egg stiffly, fold it into to the milk and serve. A teaspoon of cream added to the mixture makes a richer drink, but is not essential.

Chocolate Sauce

½ pint milk 1 dessertspoon plain drinking chocolate 1 large egg
2 teaspoons sugar

Put the milk in a pan over the heat, sprinkle in the chocolate and stir until dissolved. Break the egg into a basin, add the sugar and beat lightly. When the milk is almost, but not quite, boiling, pour on to the beaten egg, whisking while pouring and continuing for a few minutes. Put into a jug and stand in a pan of boiling water until the custard thickens.

Chocolate Custard Sauce

½ oz custard powder 1½ oz sugar
½ oz cocoa powder ½ pint milk

Mix together in a bowl the custard and cocoa powders and sugar and blend with 3 tablespoons of cold milk. Put the remaining milk into a pan, bring to the boil and, when boiling, pour on to the custard/cocoa mixture, stirring all the while. Return to the pan and simmer, stirring, for about 3 minutes until the custard thickens.

Chocolate Icing

2 oz best quality plain block chocolate **4oz icing sugar**
2 tablespoons milk and water mixed **Vanilla essence**

Roughly chop the chocolate, put it into a basin with the milk and water and stand in a pan of hot water to melt. When the chocolate has melted, stir in the icing sugar and then a few drops of vanilla essence. Beat thoroughly and when smooth and creamy use to ice eclairs, cream buns, cakes and fancies.

Chocolate Butter Icing

2 oz best quality plain block chocolate
4 oz butter **6 oz icing sugar** **Vanilla essence**

Melt the chocolate in a basin set over a pan of hot water. Cream the butter in a bowl with a wooden spoon then sieve in the icing sugar by degrees, beating well. Add a few drops of vanilla essence and then stir in the melted chocolate. Beat well until creamy and spread on the cake as required.

Chocolate Fudge Filling

1½ oz butter **3 oz plain drinking chocolate**
1 lb caster sugar **¼ pint cream or evaporated milk**
4 teaspoons vanilla essence

Put all the ingredients, except the essence, into a heavy saucepan over a low heat. Stir gently until melted then bring to the boil and continue until the mixture begins to thicken. Add the vanilla essence, beat until the mixture thickens then set aside to cool. When almost cold, spread on the cake as required.

Chocolate Banana Filling

1 teaspoon plain drinking chocolate
2 teaspoons caster sugar **5 tablespoons cream** **2 bananas**

Put the chocolate powder into a basin with the sugar and 1 or 2 tablespoons of the cream. Mix well together. Whip the remainder of the cream fairly stiffly. Peel and cut up the bananas and add the cream and the banana pieces to the chocolate mixture. Blend all the ingredients well together with a fork and spread on the cake as required.

Chocolate Nut Cream Filling

8 oz caster sugar
2 tablespoons water
¼ pint condensed milk
4 oz butter
1 oz plain drinking chocolate
1 oz chopped walnuts
Vanilla essence

Put the sugar, water, condensed milk, butter and chocolate powder into a heavy saucepan and melt over a low heat, stirring. Bring to the boil and boil, stirring, for 5 minutes. Take off the heat and allow to cool slowly, stirring in the nuts and a few drops of vanilla essence. When almost cold spread on the cake as required.

Chocolate Hungarian Filling

2 oz best quality plain block chocolate
4 oz butter
6 oz icing sugar
2 teaspoons coffee essence
White of 1 egg (note: the egg is uncooked)

Melt the chocolate in a basin set over a pan of hot water. Cream the butter in a bowl with a wooden spoon and sieve in the icing sugar and beat well. Next add the melted chocolate and the coffee essence and beat all together thoroughly until creamy. Finally, whip the egg white stiffly and fold in to the filling with a metal spoon. Spread on the cake as required.

METRIC CONVERSIONS

The weights, measures and oven temperatures used in the preceding recipes can be easily converted to their metric equivalents. The conversions listed below are only approximate, having been rounded up or down as may be appropriate.

Weights

Avoirdupois	Metric
1 oz.	just under 30 grams
4 oz. (¼ lb.)	app. 115 grams
8 oz. (½ lb.)	app. 230 grams
1 lb.	454 grams

Liquid Measures

Imperial	Metric
1 tablespoon (liquid only)	20 millilitres
1 fl. oz.	app. 30 millilitres
1 gill (¼ pt.)	app. 145 millilitres
½ pt.	app. 285 millilitres
1 pt.	app. 570 millilitres
1 qt.	app. 1.140 litres

Oven Temperatures

	°Fahrenheit	Gas Mark	°Celsius
Slow	300	2	150
	325	3	170
Moderate	350	4	180
	375	5	190
	400	6	200
Hot	425	7	220
	450	8	230
	475	9	240

Flour as specified in these recipes refers to plain flour unless otherwise described.